THE STATIONS

OR THE HOLY WAY OF THE CROSS

REV. BERNARD O'REILLY

ALICIA EDITIONS

CONTENTS

THE ANTIPHON.

We beseech Thee, O Lord! to assist and direct our actions by Thy powerful grace, and all our prayers and works may always begin and end with Thee. Through Christ our Lord. Amen.

A PREPARATORY ACT OF CONTRITION.

O Jesus, treasure of my soul, infinitely good, infinitely merciful, behold me prostrate at Thy sacred feet! Sinner as I am, I fly to the arms of Thy mercy, and implore that grace which melts and converts — the grace of true compunction. I have offended Thee, adorable Jesus! I repent; let the favor of my love equal the baseness of my ingratitude. This Way of the Cross, grant me to offer devoutly in memory of that painful journey Thou hast travelled for our redemption, to the Cross of Calvary, with the holy design to reform my morals, amend my life and gain these indulgences granted by Thy vicars on earth. I apply one for my miserable soul, the rest in suffrage for the souls in purgatory, particularly N. N. [Here mention the souls for whom you intend to apply them.] I begin this devotion under Thy sacred protection, and in imitation of Thy dolorous Mother. Let then this holy exercise obtain for me mercy in this life, and glory in the next. Amen. Jesus!

Christ is sentenced to death by Pilate.

STATION I

CHRIST IS SENTENCED TO DEATH BY PILATE.

V. We adore Thee, O Lord Jesus Christ, and bless Thee.
R. Because by Thy holy Cross Thou hast redeemed the world.

The Mystery.

OUR gracious Redeemer, after suffering blows and blasphemies before Annas and Caiphas, after the cruel scourging, insulting contempts and bloody crown of piercing thorns, is unjustly condemned to death. This iniquitous sentence your Jesus accepted with admirable humility. Innocence embraces condemnation to free the guilty. Reflect that your sins were the false witnesses that condemned Him; your stubborn impenitence the tyrant that extorted from Pilate the bloody sentence. Propose now seriously an amendment of life, and while you reflect on the horrid injustice of Pilate, who condemns innocence, lest he should not appear a friend of Caesar, arraign yourself for your many sins of human respect; think how often you have offended God for fear of displeasing the eye of the world, and turning to your loving Jesus, address Him rather with tears of the heart than with expressions of the tongue in the following

Prayer.

O Mangled victim of my sins! O suffering Jesus! I have deserved those bloody scourges, that cruel sentence of death; and yet Thou didst die for me, that I should live for Thee. I am convinced that if I desire to please men, I cannot be Thy servant. Let me then displease the world and its vain admirers. I resign myself into Thy hands. Let love take possession of my heart; let Thy eyes behold with contempt everything that can alienate my affections from Thee; let my ears be ever attentive to Thy word; let me through this painful journey accompany Thee, sighing and demanding mercy. Mercy! Jesus! Amen.

Our Father, &c. Hail Mary, &c.

Jesus Christ crucified, have
mercy on us!
You pious Christians who do
now draw near.
With relenting hearts now lend
a tear.
Your Lord behold with great
humility.
Sentenced to die on Mount
Calvary.

Station II.

Christ takes the Cross on his shoulder.

STATION II

CHRIST TAKES THE CROSS ON HIS SHOULDER

V. We adore Thee, O Lord Jesus Christ, and bless Thee.
R. Because by Thy holy Cross Thou has redeemed the world.

The Mystery.

THIS second Station represents the place where your most amiable Redeemer is clad in his usual attire, after His inhuman executioners had stripped Him of the purple garment of derision with which He was clothed, when as a visionary king they crowned Him with plaited thorns. The heavy burthen of the

Cross Is violently placed on His mangled shoulders.

Behold your gracious Saviour, though torn with wounds, covered with blood, a man of griefs, abandoned by all — with what silent patience He bears the taunts and injuries with which the Jews insult Him. He stretches out His bleeding arms, and tenderly embraces the Cross. Reflect with confusion on that sensitive pride which is fired with impatience at the very shadow of contempt — on your discontented murmurs in your lightest afflictions — and your obstinate resistance to the will of Heaven in the crosses of life, which are calculated to conduct you not to a Calvary of Crucifixion, but to joys of eternal glory; and from your heart unite in the following

Prayer.

MEEK AND HUMBLE Jesus! my iniquity and perverseness loaded Thy shoulders with the heavy burthen of the Cross. Yet I, a vile worm of the earth, O shameful ingratitude! fly even the appearance of mortification, and everything which would check the violence of my passions;

and if I suffered, it was with a murmuring reluctance. I now, O Saviour of the world! detest my past life, and by Thy grace am determined no more to offend Thee mortally. Let me only glory in the Cross of my Lord, by whom the world is crucified to me, and I to the world. Lay then on my stubborn neck the cross of true penance; let me, for the love of Thee, bear the adversities of this life, and cleave inseparably to Thee in the bonds of perpetual charity. Amen. Jesus.

Our Father, &c. Hail Mary, &c. Glory, &c.

Jesus Christ crucified, have mercy on us!

No pity for the Lamb was to be
found;
As a mock King my loving
Lord they crown'd.
To bear the heavy cross He
does not tire,
To save my soul from ever-
lasting fire.

Station III.

Jesus falls the first time under the Cross.

STATION III

JESUS FALLS THE FIRST TIME
UNDER THE CROSS.

V. We adore Thee, O Lord Jesus Christ, and bless Thee.
R. Because by Thy holy Cross Thou hast redeemed the world.

The Mystery.

THIS third Station represents how our Lord Jesus Christ, overwhelmed by the weight of the Cross, fainting through loss of blood, falls to the ground the first time.

Contemplate the unwearied patience of the meek Lamb, amidst the insulting blows and curses of His brutal executioners; while you, impatient in adversity and infirmity, presume to complain, nay, to insult the Majesty of Heaven, by your curses and blasphemies. Purpose here firmly to struggle against the impatient sallies of temper; and beholding your amiable Jesus prostrate under the Cross, excite in yourself a just hatred for those sins, which rendered insupportable that weight, with which your Saviour, for love of you, was burthened, and thus address your afflicted Jesus:

Prayer.

ALAS, MY Jesus! the merciless violence of Thy inhuman executioners, the excessive weight of the Cross, or rather the more oppressive load of my sins, crush Thee to the earth. Panting for breath, exhausted as Thou art. Thou dost not refuse new tortures for me. Will I then refuse the light burthen of Thy commandments; will I refuse to do violence to my perverse passions and sinful attachments; will I relapse into those very crimes for which I have shed false and delusive tears! O Jesus! stretch Thy holy hand to my assistance, that I may never more fall into mortal sin; that I may at the hour of death secure the important affair of my salvation. Amen, Jesus.

Our Father, &c. Hail Mary, &c. Glory, &c.

Jesus Christ crucified, have mercy on us!

*From loss of blood He fell unto
    the ground.
No comfort for my Lord was to
    be found,
He rose again beneath their
    cruel blows,
And on His bitter way un-
    murmering goes.*

Station IV.

Jesus carrying the Cross, meets his most afflicted Mother.

STATION IV

JESUS CARRYING THE CROSS, MEETS HIS MOST AFFLICTED MOTHER.

V. We adore Thee, O Lord Jesus Christ, and bless Thee.
R. Because by Thy holy Cross Thou hast redeemed the world.

The Mystery.

THE fourth Station represents to your contemplation the meeting of the desolate Mother and her bleeding Jesus, staggering under the weight of the Cross. Consider what pangs rent her soul, when she beheld her beloved Jesus covered with blood, dragged violently to the place of execution, reviled and blasphemed by an ungrateful, outrageous rabble. Meditate on her inward feelings, the looks of silent agony exchanged between the Mother and the Son; her anguish in not being permitted to approach, to embrace and to accompany Him to death. Filled with confusion at the thought that neither the Son's pains nor Mother's grief have softened the hardness of your heart, contritely join in the following.

Prayer.

O MARY! I am the cause of thy sufferings. O refuge of sinners! let me participate in those heart-felt pangs, which rent thy tender soul, when thou didst behold thy Son trembling with cold, covered with wounds, fainting under the Cross, more dead than alive! Mournful Mother! fountain of love! let me feel the force of thy grief that I may weep with thee, and mingle my tears with thine, and thy Son's blood. O suffering Jesus! by Thy bitter passion, and the heart-breaking compassion of Thy afflicted Mother, grant me the efficacious grace of perseverance! Mother of Jesus, intercede for me! Jesus, behold me with, an eye of pity, and in the hour of my

death receive me to the arms of Thy mercy!
Amen, Jesus.

Our Father, &c. Hail Mary, &c.
Glory, &c.

Jesus Christ crucified, have mercy on us!

Exhausted, spent, see Jesus
onward go,
With feeble step, in anguish
faint and slow.
At last His grief-worn Mother
He can see
Exclaiming: My Son, my heart
is rent for Thee.

STATION V.

CHRIST ASSISTED BY SIMON THE CYRENEAN TO CARRY THE CROSS.

STATION V

CHRIST ASSISTED BY SIMON THE CYRENEAN TO CARRY THE CROSS.

V. We adore Thee, O Lord Jesus Christ, and bless Thee.

R. Because by Thy holy Cross Thou hast redeemed the world.

The Mystery.

THE fifth Station represents Christ fainting, destitute of strength, unable to carry the Cross. His sacrilegious executioners compel Simon the Cyrenean, to carry it, not through compassionate pity to Jesus, but lest he should expire in their hand, before they could glut their vengeance by nailing Him to the Cross. Consider here the repugnance of

Simon to carry the Cross after Christ; and that you with repugnance, and by compulsion, carry the Cross which Providence has placed on your shoulders. Will you spurn the love of your Jesus, who invites you to take up your Cross and follow Him? Will you yet with shameless ingratitude refuse the Cross, sanctified by His suffering? Offer up devoutly the following.

Prayer.

O SUFFERING Jesus! to what excess did Thy impious executioners' cruelty proceed! Beholding Thee faint under the Cross, apprehensive of Thy death before they could complete their bloody intentions, they compel Simon to carry the Cross that Thou mightest expire on it in the most exquisite torture. But why should I complain of the cruelty of the Jews or the repugnance of Simon? Have I not again crucified Thee by my crimes? Have I not suffered with fretful impatience the light afflictions with which Thy mercy visited me? Inspire me now, my Jesus, to detest and deplore my sinful impatience, my ungrateful murmurs, and let me with all my heart cheerfully accompany Thee to Mount Calvary; let me live in Thee, and die in Thee. Amen, Jesus.

Our Father, &c. Hail Mary, &c. Glory, &c.

Jesus Christ crucified, have mercy on us!

The furious Jews when Jesus
    fainting fell
Simon to bear His Cross, by
    force compel;
Afflictions bear like Job most
    patiently,
And follow the Lamb with
    great humility.

Station VI.

VERONICA PRESENTS A HANDKERCHIEF TO CHRIST.

STATION VI

VERONICA PRESENTS A HANDKERCHIEF TO CHRIST.

V. We adore Thee, O Lord Jesus Christ, and bless Thee.
R. Because by Thy holy Cross Thou hast redeemed the world.

The Mystery.

THE sixth Station represents the place where the pious Veronica, compassionating our agonizing Redeemer, beholding His sacred face livid with blows and covered with blood and sweat, presents a handkerchief, with which Jesus wipes his face. Consider the heroic piety of this devout woman, who is not intimidated by the presence of the executioners, or the clamors of the Jews; and the tender acknowledgment of Jesus. Reflect here, that though you cannot personally discharge the debt of humanity to your Saviour, you can discharge it to His suffering members, the poor. Though you cannot wipe away the blood and sweat from the face of Jesus, you can wipe away the tear of wretchedness from the eye of misery. Examine, then, what returns you have made for the singular graces and favors your bountiful Jesus bestowed on you; and conscious of your ingratitude, address your injured Saviour in the following.

Prayer.

O JESUS, grant me tears to weep my ingratitude. How often have I, infatuated wretch, turned my eyes from Thee and Thy sufferings, to fix them on the world and its vanities! Let me henceforth be Thine without division. Stamp Thy image on my soul, that it may never admit another love. Take possession of my heart on earth, that my soul may take eternal possession of Thee in glory. Amen, Jesus!

Our Father, &c. Hail Mary, &c.
Glory, &c.

Jesus Christ crucified, have mercy on us!

Veronica pressed through to
meet our Lord,
His streaming face a napkin to
afford,
Lo, on its texture stamped by
power divine
His sacred features breathe in
every line.

Jesus falls under the Cross the second time.

STATION VII

JESUS FALLS UNDER THE CROSS THE SECOND TIME.

V. We adore Thee, O Lord Jesus Christ, and bless Thee.

R. Because by Thy holy Cross Thou hast redeemed the world.

The Mystery.

THE seventh Station represents the gate of Jerusalem, called the gate of Judgment, at the entrance of which our Saviour, through anguish and weakness, falls to the ground. He is compelled by blows and blasphemies to rise.

Consider your Jesus prostrate on the earth, bruised by His fall, and ignominiously treated by an ungrateful rabble. Reflect that your self-love and pride of preference were the cause of this humiliation. Implore, then, grace to detest sincerely your haughty spirit and proud disposition. It was your reiterated sins which again pressed Him to the ground. Will you then sin again, and add to the afflictions of your gracious Saviour?

Prayer.

O MOST Holy Redeemer! treated with the utmost contempt, deprived of fame and honor — led out to punishment — through excess of torments, and the weakness of Thy delicate and mangled body, Thou didst fall a second time to the earth. What impious hand has prostrated Thee? Alas, my Jesus! I am that impious, that sacrilegious offender: my ambitious pride, my haughty indignation, my contempt of others humbled Thee to the earth. Banish for ever from my mind the unhappy spirit of pride. Teach my heart the doctrine of humility, so that detesting pride, vain glory and human respect, I may forever be united with Thee, my meek and humble Jesus. Amen.

Our Father, &c. Hail Mary, &c. Glory, &c.

Jesus Christ crucified, have mercy on us!

Prone at the city gate He fell
 once more,
To save our erring souls He
 suffered sore;
On His great mercy let us al-
 ways call,
Since our vain pride has
 caused His triple fall.

Christ consoles the Women of Jerusalem who wept over him.

STATION VIII

CHRIST CONSOLES THE WOMEN OF JERUSALEM, WHO WEPT OVER HIM.

V. We adore Thee O Lord Jesus Christ, and bless Thee.

R. Because by Thy holy Cross Thou hast redeemed the world.

The Mystery.

THIS Station represents the place where several devout women meeting Jesus, and beholding Him wounded and bathed in His blood, shed tears of compassion over Him.

Consider the excessive love of Jesus, who, though languishing and half dead through the multitude of His torments, is nevertheless attentive to console the women who wept over Him. They merited that tender consolation from the mouth of Jesus, " Weep not over me, but over yourselves and your children." Weep for your sins, the sources of my affliction. Yes, O my soul! I will obey my suffering Lord, and pour out tears of compunction. Nothing more eloquent than the voice of those tears which flow from the horror of those sins. Address Him the following

Prayer.

O JESUS, ONLY BEGOTTEN Son of the Father! who will give water to my head, and a fountain of tears to my eyes, that I may day and night weep and lament my sins? I humbly beseech Thee by these tears of blood Thou didst shed for me, to soften my flinty bosom, that tears may plentifully flow from my eyes, and contrition rend my heart, this hardened heart, to cancel my crimes and render me secure in the day of wrath and examination, when Thou wilt come to judge the living and the dead, and demand a rigorous account of Thy blood. Amen, Jesus.

Our Father, &c. Hail Mary, &c. Glory, &c.

Jesus Christ crucified, have mercy on us!

With tears of love the women
they did weep.
Compassionating our Re-
deemer sweet;
Weep for your sins who caused
Him here to be
O Lamb of God Thy mercy
show to me.

JESUS FALLS UNDER THE CROSS THE THIRD TIME.

STATION IX

JESUS FALLS UNDER THE CROSS
THE THIRD TIME.

V. We adore Thee, O Lord Jesus Christ, and bless Thee.

R. Because by Thy holy Cross Thou hast redeemed the world.

The Mystery.

THIS Station represents the foot of Mount Calvary, where Jesus Christ, quite destitute of strength, falls a third time to the ground. The anguish of His wounds is renewed.

Consider here the many Injuries and blasphemous derisions thrown out against Christ, to compel Him to rise and hasten to the place of execution, that His inveterate enemies might enjoy the savage satisfaction of beholding Him expire on the Cross. Consider that by your sins you daily hurry Him to the place of execution. Approach Him in thought to the foot of Mount Calvary, and cry out against the accursed weight of sin that prostrated Jesus, and had long since buried thee in the flames of hell, if His mercy and the merits of His passion had not preserved thee.

Prayer.

O CLEMENT Jesus! I return Thee infinite thanks for not permitting me, ungrateful sinner, as Thou has permitted thousands less criminal, to die in their sins. I, who have added torments to Thy torments, by heaping sin on sin, kindle in my soul the fire of charity, fan it with Thy continual grace into perseverance, until, delivered from the body of this death, I can enjoy the liberty of the children of God and Thy co-heirs. Amen, Jesus!

Our Father, &c. Hail Mary, &c. Glory, &c.

Jesus Christ crucified, have mercy on us!

*On Calvary's height a third
time see Him fall,
Livid with bruises that our
sight appal.
O gracious Lord, this sufferedst Thou for me.
To save my soul from endless
misery.*

STATION X.

JESUS IS STRIPPED OF HIS GARMENTS AND OFFERED VINEGAR AND GALL.

STATION X

JESUS IS STRIPPED OF HIS GARMENTS, AND OFFERED VINEGAR AND GALL.

V. We adore Thee, O Lord Jesus Christ, and bless Thee.
R. Because by Thy holy Cross Thou hast redeemed the world.

The Mystery.

THIS Station represents how our Lord Jesus Christ ascended Mount Calvary, and was by His inhuman executioners stripped of His garments. The skin and congealed blood are torn off with them, and His wounds renewed.

Consider the confusion of the modest Lamb, exposed naked to the contempt and derision of an insulting rabble. They present Him with vinegar and gall for a refreshment. Condemn here that delicacy of taste, that sensual indulgence, with which you flatter your sinful body. Pray here for the spirit of Christian mortification. Think how happy you would die if, stripped of the world and its attachments, you could expire covered with the blood and agony of Jesus.

Prayer.

Suffering Jesus! I behold Thee stript of Thy garments, Thy old wounds renewed, and new ones added to the old. I behold Thee naked in the presence of thousands, exposed to the inclemency of the weather; cold, trembling from head to foot, insulted by the blasphemous derisions of the spectators. Strip, O mangled Lamb of God! my heart of the world and its deceitful affections. Divest my soul of its habits of sensual indulgence. Embitter the poisoned cup of pleasure, that I may dash it with contempt from my lips, and through Christian mortification arrive at Thy never fading glory. Amen, Jesus.

Our Father, &c. Hail Mary, &c. Glory, &c.

Jesus Christ crucified, have mercy on us!

O Queen of angels, how thy
heart did bleed
To see thy Son stripped naked
here indeed,
And to the vile and cruel
throng exposed,
Who round Him now in furious
hatred closed

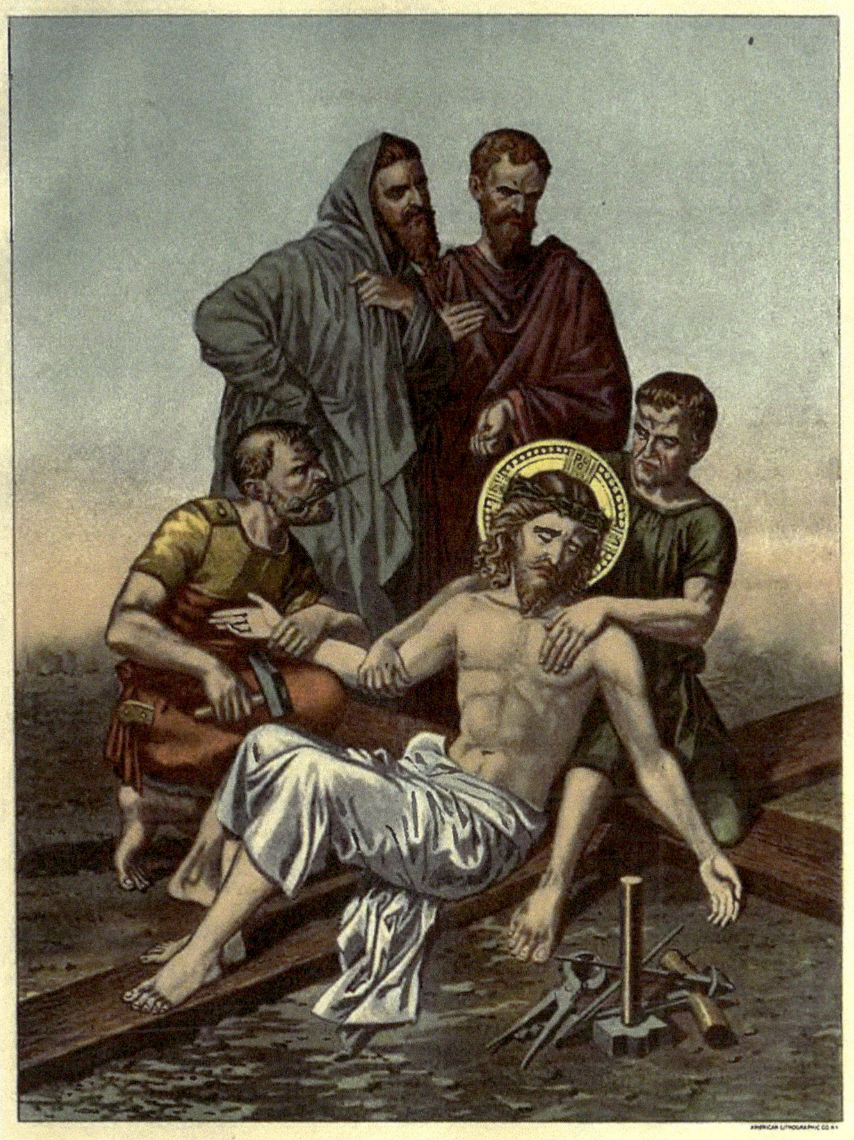

JESUS IS NAILED TO THE CROSS.

STATION XI

CHRIST IS NAILED TO THE CROSS.

V. We adore Thee, O Lord Jesus Christ, and bless Thee.

R. Because by Thy holy Cross Thou hast redeemed the world.

The Mystery.

THIS Station represents the place where Jesus Christ, in the presence of His afflicted mother, is stretched on the Cross, and nailed to it. How insufferable the torture — the nerves and sinews are rent by the nails.

Consider the exceeding desolation, the anguish of the tender Mother, eye-witness of this inhuman punishment of her beloved Jesus. Generously resolve then to crucify your criminal desires, and nail your sins to the wood of the Cross. Contemplate the suffering resignation of the Son of God to the will of His Father, while you are impatient in trifling afflictions, in trivial disappointments. Purpose henceforth to embrace your cross with ready resignation to the will of God.

Prayer.

O PATIENT Jesus! meek Lamb of God! who promised, " When I shall be exalted from earth I will draw all things to myself," attract my heart to Thee, and nail it to the Cross. I now renounce and detest my past impatience.

Let me crucify my flesh with its concupiscence and vices. Here burn, here cut, but spare me for eternity. I throw myself into the arms of Thy mercy. Thy will be done in all things Grant me resignation, grant me Thy love, I desire no more. Amen, Jesus.

Our Father, &c. Hail Mary, &c. Glory, &c.

Jesus Christ crucified, have mercy on us!

You Christian hearts now join
with Mary's grief;
Heaven and earth behold!
deny relief;
Her heart was pierced with
bitter grief to see
Her loving Jesus nailed unto a
tree.

CHRIST IS EXALTED ON THE CROSS AND DIES.

STATION XII

CHRIST IS EXALTED ON THE CROSS AND DIES.

V. We adore Thee, O Lord Jesus Christ, and bless Thee.
R. Because by Thy holy Cross Thou hast redeemed the world.

The Mystery.

THIS Station represents the place where Jesus Christ was publicly exalted on the Cross between two robbers, who, for their enormous crimes, were executed with the innocent Lamb.

Consider here the confusion of your Saviour, exposed naked to the profane view of a blasphemous multitude. Imagine yourself at the foot of the Cross. Behold that sacred body streaming blood from every part. Contemplate the divine countenance pale and languid, the heart throbbing in the last pangs of agony, the soul on the point of separation; yet charity triumphs over His agony; His last prayers petition forgiveness for His enemies: "Father, forgive them, for they know not what they do." His clemency is equally extended to the penitent thief: " This day shalt thou be with me in Paradise." He recommends in His last moments His disconsolate Mother to His beloved St. John. He recommends His soul to His heavenly Father, and bowing down His submissive, obedient head, resigns His spirit. Turn your eyes on the naked, bloody portrait of charity. Number His wounds. Wash them with tears of sympathizing love. Behold the arms extended to embrace you. Love of Jesus! thou diest to deliver us from eternal captivity.

Prayer.

O SUFFERING Son of God! I now behold Thee in the last convulsive pangs of death — Thy veins opened. Thy sinews torn. Thy hands and feet, O Fountain of Paradise!

distilling blood. I acknowledge, charitable Jesus, that my reiterated offences have been Thy merciless executioners, the cause of Thy bitter sufferings and death. Yet, God of mercy, look on my sinful soul, bathe it in Thy precious blood! Let me die to the vanity of the world, and renounce its false pleasures. Thou didst pray, my Jesus, for Thy enemies. I forgive mine. I embrace them in the bowels of Thy charity. I bury my resentment in Thy wounds. Shelter me in the day of wrath in the sanctuary of Thy side. Let me live, let me die, in my crucified Jesus. Amen.

Our Father, &c. Hail Mary, &c. Glory, &c.

Jesus Christ crucified, have mercy on us!

Behold the streams of blood
from every part,
Behold the sharp lance that
pierc'd His Sacred Heart;
On Calvary's Mount behold
Him naked hang,
To suffer for our sins pain's ut-
most pang.

Station XIII.

Christ is taken down from the Cross.

STATION XIII

CHRIST IS TAKEN DOWN FROM THE CROSS.

V. We adore Thee, O Lord Jesus Christ, and bless Thee.

R. Because by Thy holy Cross Thou hast redeemed the world.

The Mystery.

THIS Station represents the place where Christ's most sacred body was taken down from the Cross by Joseph and Nicodemus, and laid in the bosom of His weeping Mother.

Consider the sighs and tears of the Virgin Mother, with what pangs she embraced the bloody remains of her beloved Jesus. Here unite your tears with those of the disconsolate Mother. Reflect that your Jesus would not descend from the Cross until He consummated the work of redemption; and that at His departure from, as well as at His entrance into the world, He would be placed in the bosom of His beloved Mother. Hence learn constancy in your pious resolutions! cleave to the standard of the Cross. Consider with what purity that soul should be adorned which receives, in the blessed Sacrament of the Eucharist, Christ's most sacred body and blood.

Prayer.

AT LENGTH, O Blessed Virgin ! Mother of sorrow! thou art permitted to embrace thy beloved Son. But alas! the fruit of thy immaculate womb is all over mangled, in one continued wound. Yes, O Lord! the infernal fury of the Jews has at length triumphed; yet we renew their barbarity, crucifying Thee by our sins, inflicting new wounds. Most afflicted mother of my Redeemer, I conjure thee by the pains and torments thou sufferedst in the common cause of Salvation, to obtain for me, by thy powerful intercession, pardon of my sins, and grace to weep with a sympathizing feeling, thine and thy Son's afflictions. As often as I appear at the Holy Sacrifice of the Mass, let me embrace Tliee, my Jesus, in the bosom of my heart. May I worthily receive Thee as the sacred pledge of my salvation. Amen, Jesus.

Our Father, &c. Hail Mary, &c. Glory, &c.

Jesus Christ crucified, have mercy on us!

*When from the Cross they took
    this blessed form.
His Mother cries, my Son, I am
    forlorn;
My child is dead, you virgins
    join with me.
Bewail in tears my love's sad
    destiny.*

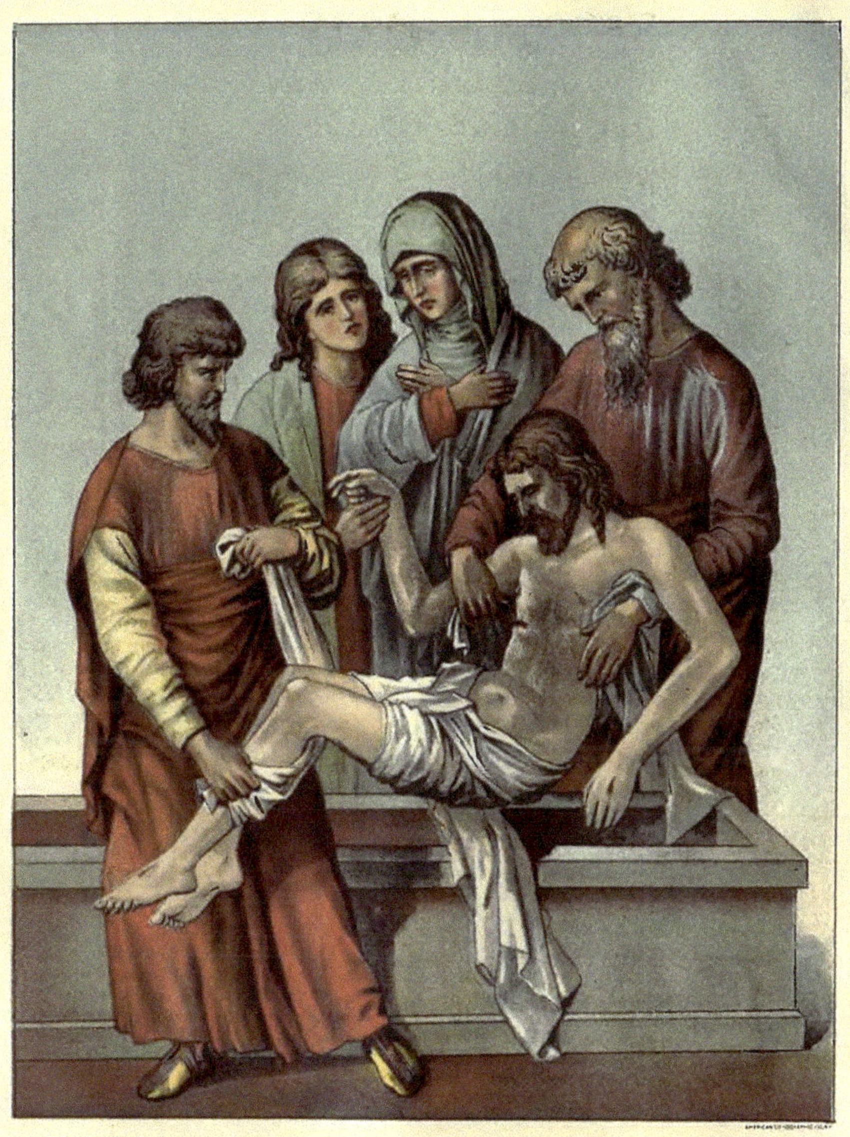

CHRIST IS LAID IN THE HOLY SEPULCHRE.

STATION XIV

CHRIST IS LAID IN THE HOLY SEPULCHRE.

V. We adore Thee, O Lord Jesus Christ, and bless Thee.

R. Because by Thy holy Cross Thou hast redeemed the world.

The Mystery.

THIS Station represents Christ's Sepulchre, where His blessed body was laid with piety and devotion.

Consider the emotions of the Virgin — her eyes streaming with tears, her bosom heaving with sighs. What melancholy, what wistful looks she cast on that monument where the treasure of her soul, her Jesus, her all, lay entombed. Here lament your want of contrition for your sins, and humbly adore your deceased Lord, who, poor even in death, is buried in another's tomb. Blush at your dependence on the world, and the eager solicitude with which you labor to grasp its perishable advantages. Despise henceforth the world, lest you perish with it.

Prayer.

CHARITABLE Jesus, for my salvation Thou performedst the painful journey of the Cross. Let me press the footsteps marked by Thee, gracious Redeemer — the paths which, through the thorns of life, conduct to the heavenly Jerusalem. Would that Thou wert entombed in my heart, that being united to Thee, I might rise to a new life of grace, and persevere to the end. Grant me, in my last moments, to receive Thy precious Body, as the pledge of immortal life. Let my last words be Jesus and Mary, my last breath be united to Thy last breath on the Cross; that with a lively faith, a firm hope and ardent love, I may die with Thee and for Thee; that I may reign with Thee for ever and ever. Amen, Jesus.

Our Father, &c. Hail Mary, &c. Glory, &c.

Jesus Christ crucified, have mercy on us!

You pious Christians, raise
your voices, raise,
And join with me to sing your
Saviour's praise.
Who shed His blood for us and
died in pain.
To save our souls from hell's
eternal flame.

CONCLUSION

COMPASSIONATE Jesus! behold with eyes of mercy this devotion I have endeavored to perform, in honor of Thy bitter passion and death, in order to obtain remission of my sins, and the pains incurred by them. Accept of it for the salvation of the living and the eternal repose of the faithful departed, particularly for those for whom I directed it. Do not, my Jesus, suffer the ineffable price of Thy blood to be fruitless, nor my miserable soul ransomed by it, to perish. The voice of Thy blood is louder for mercy than my crimes for vengeance. Have mercy then, O Lord! have mercy, and spare me for Thy mercy's sake! Amen, Jesus.